A Character Building Book™

Learning About Achievement From the Life of
Maya Angelou

Brenn Jones

The Rosen Publishing Group's
PowerKids Press™
New York

To Maelstrom and Fee

Published in 2002 by The Rosen Publishing Group, Inc.
29 East 21st Street, New York, NY 10010

First Edition

Book Design: Michael Caroleo

Project Editor: Emily Raabe

Photo Credits: p. 4 Mitchell Gerber/CORBIS; p. 7 © CORBIS; p. 8 © Reuters NewMedia Inc./CORBIS; pp. 11, 12, 15, 19 © Bettmann/CORBIS; p. 21 © Leif Skoogfors/CORBIS.

Jones, Brenn.
    Learning about achievement from the life of Maya Angelou / Brenn Jones. −1st ed.
        p. cm. −(A character building book)
Includes index.
    ISBN 0-8239-5780-2 (lib. bdg.)
    1. Angelou, Maya—Juvenile literature. 2. Authors, American—20th century—Biography —Juvenile literature. 3. Afro-American women civil rights workers—Biography—Juvenile literature. 4. Women entertainers—United States—Biography—Juvenile literature. [1. Angelou, Maya. 2. Authors, American. 3. Afro-Americans—Biography. 4. Women—Biography.]
I. Title. II. Series.
    PS3551.N464 Z7 2002
    818'.5409—dc21

                                                                                                    00-012004
                                                                                                    CIP

Manufactured in the United States of America

Contents

Achievement

When you achieve something, you reach a goal toward which you have worked. Maya Angelou has achieved many things in her life. She has written books of poetry, **autobiographies**, children's books, and **screenplays**. Maya also has achieved other things. She has been a singer, actress, and movie director. She has been a professor at several universities and has worked for **civil rights** both in the United States and in Africa. Maya has raised a son, and she is a great-grandmother.

◀ *Many people have gotten to know and love Maya through her achievements.*

Stamps, Arkansas

Maya was born in St. Louis, Missouri, on April 4, 1928. Her name was Marguerite Johnson but her brother Bailey called her "My sister." He changed that to "My" and then to "Maya," which is the name that she chose to keep. When she was three years old, Maya's parents got divorced. Maya and Bailey went to live with their grandmother Annie Henderson in Stamps, Arkansas. Annie owned a small grocery store. People in the neighborhood met at the store to give haircuts, tell stories, and gossip with each other.

This is St. Louis, Missouri, where Maya was born. ▶

Maya
Angelou

I Know
Why
the Caged
Bird Sings

New York Times Bestselling Author of *The Heart of a Woman*

Love of Reading

While she was growing up, Maya loved to read. Maya's favorite writers were William Shakespeare, Paul Laurence Dunbar, Langston Hughes, and W. E. B. DuBois. Maya's grandmother had a friend named Bertha Flowers. Bertha told Maya to listen carefully to the storytellers in the neighborhood. She also helped Maya practice reading aloud. By doing these things, Maya learned to tell stories very well.

In 1941, Maya left Stamps to live with her mother in San Francisco, California.

◀ *This is Maya, and a picture of a book she wrote called* I Know Why the Caged Bird Sings.

San Francisco

Maya went to high school in San Francisco. After she graduated, Maya had a son, named Guy. Maya worked hard to support herself and Guy. When she was 17, Maya became the first African American streetcar conductor on San Francisco's Market Street Railway. She also worked as a cook, a dancer, and a singer. While she was working as a singer in a nightclub, Maya met the famous singer Billie Holiday. Billie told Maya that she would be famous someday.

10 *This is Maya, dancing on a beach while visiting San Francisco in 1970. Although Maya did not live in San Francisco after 1957, she returned to visit many times.* ▶

Civil Rights

In 1957, Maya and Guy moved to New York City. There, Maya helped Martin Luther King Jr., and his Southern Christian Leadership Conference (known as the SCLC) fight against **racism**. Maya raised money for the SCLC with a show called Cabaret for Freedom. She wrote, directed, and starred in the show. Maya also became one of the leaders in the SCLC.

Maya began to focus on her writing in New York. She published her first short story in a journal called *Revolución* in 1958.

◄ *This is Martin Luther King Jr., who was a famous leader for civil rights. Martin and the SCLC led marches through New York City streets to help gain equality for African Americans.*

Africa

In the early 1960s, Maya moved again. She lived in the African countries of Egypt and Ghana. Maya met another powerful civil rights leader in Ghana. His name was Malcolm X. When Maya went back to the United States in 1965, she wanted to help Malcolm X. Two days after Maya returned to the United States, though, Malcolm X was killed. Maya decided that she would help African Americans achieve equality through her writing. She decided to write books about being an African American.

In Egypt, Maya edited the Arab Observer, *an English language newspaper. In Ghana, Maya worked at the University of Ghana* ▶ *and wrote for the* Ghanaian Times.

Writing

In 1970, Maya wrote an autobiography of her childhood in Stamps, Arkansas. The book was called *I Know Why the Caged Bird Sings*. Maya wrote about her years in Africa in two other books, *The Heart of a Woman* and *All God's Children Need Traveling Shoes*. In 1971, Maya published her first book of poetry, *Just Give Me a Cool Drink of Water 'fore I Die*. Maya has written many books for children. She also has worked on films and in theater. In 1972, Maya wrote the script for a movie called *Georgia, Georgia*.

◀ *This is Maya in Los Angeles in 1998. She is directing a film called* On the Delta.

Maya's Routine

Writers write in many different places. Some writers work in an office, some like to write in a quiet park, and some like to write at home in the middle of the night. Maya writes in a hotel room. She wakes up about 5:30 in the morning and goes to a hotel near her home. She brings a yellow pad of paper, a **thesaurus**, a Bible, something to drink, and playing cards to the hotel room. Sometimes when Maya is writing, she stops to play a game of cards. Playing cards helps Maya organize her stories in her head.

Maya travels a lot to give speeches. She is also a professor of American Studies at Wake Forest University in North Carolina. ▶

Honors

The National Book Award and the Pulitzer Prize are two of the highest honors that can be given to a writer. The Tony Award is one of the greatest awards that an actress or actor can win. Maya has been nominated for all three of these awards! She also has been granted **honorary degrees** from several colleges and universities. When Bill Clinton became president in 1993, he asked Maya to read her poem "On the Pulse of Morning" at his **inauguration**. Millions of people watched as Maya read.

◀ *This is President Bill Clinton and Maya at his inauguration in 1993. The recording of Maya reading her poem won the 1994 Grammy Award for best Non-Musical Album.*

In Her Own Words

In her poem "Caged Bird," Angelou writes about a bird in a cage who sings about freedom. During the difficult parts of her life, Maya sometimes felt like a caged bird. Friends such as Bertha Flowers helped Maya to believe in herself and become a great writer. Writing was a way for Maya to find freedom from the difficulties in her life. The greatest of Maya's achievements, however, is the effect that her writing has had on millions of readers. Maya's writing **inspires** other people to achieve their own dreams.

Glossary

autobiographies (aw-toh-by-AH-gruh-feez) Stories of a person's life written by that person.

civil rights (SIH-vul RYTS) The rights of all citizens.

honorary degrees (ON-er-AIR-ee duh-GREEZ) Awards given by colleges and universities to people who have made great achievements.

inauguration (ih-naw-gyuh-RAY-shun) A ceremony to begin something.

inspires (in-SPYRS) Fills people with excitement.

racism (RAY-siz-im) Dislike of other races.

screenplays (SKREEN-playz) The written stories of movies.

thesaurus (thi-SORE-us) A book that groups together similar words.

Index

Web Sites

To learn more about Maya Angelou and her achievements, check
out these Web sites:

http://www.empirezine.com/spotlight/maya/maya1.htm

http://www.mayaangelou.com